Marley and the Monkey

(A Book About ADHD)

written by
Holly Duhig

Illustratred by
Drue Rintoul

HEALTHY
MINDS

BookLife
PUBLISHING

©2019
BookLife Publishing
King's Lynn
Norfolk PE30 4LS

A catalogue record for this
book is available from the
British Library.

ISBN: 978-1-78637-357-1

Written by:
Holly Duhig

Edited by:
Kirsty Holmes

Designed & Illustrated by:
Drue Rintoul

With grateful thanks to Place2Be for their endorsement of this series.

These titles have been developed to support teachers and
school counsellors in exploring pupils' mental health, and have
been reviewed and approved by the clinical team at Place2Be,
the leading national children's mental health charity.

Something to think about...

While you're reading, have a think about these questions...

Monkey has been keeping Marley awake. Monkey jumps on the bed and swings from the lamp shade. Marley says, "Get down!" but Monkey always wants to play at bedtime.

Marley wants to play too, but he knows he'll be in trouble if Mum hears him out of bed.

"Ooh ooh ooh!" squeals Monkey. "Let's play downstairs! We can play video games!" Playing downstairs sounds like lots of fun, but Marley really doesn't want to wake Mum. He climbs back into bed even though he still feels wide awake.

The next morning, Marley is very tired. Monkey has made a real mess of his room. It's going to take Marley ages to pack his school bag. He doesn't want to get in trouble for losing his homework again.

Before they go to school, Monkey wants to watch TV. Marley is worried they don't have time.

Having a monkey is like having a watch that's always set to the wrong time. Marley doesn't want to be late for school again.

"Time to go Marley," calls his mum. Monkey jumps in Marley's school bag. He wants to go too.

At school, Marley is trying to concentrate on his lesson, but Monkey is distracting him. He won't sit still and Marley can see him jumping up and down out of the corner of his eye. Marley is jealous of Monkey; he wants to be having fun too.

Monkey tickles Marley's feet and wiggles his legs. "Come and play!"

"Stop fidgeting, Marley!" bellows Mr Robinson. Marley wishes he could tell him it's Monkey making him fidget.

Marley tries to keep still and listen to Mr Robinson but Monkey has other ideas. "Ooh ooh ooh!" says Monkey every time he has a new thought.

Having a monkey is like having a bus driver who is always trying to steer in the wrong direction.

When Mr Robinson asks the class to hand in their homework, Marley remembers he left it at home. Mr Robinson looks very disappointed. Marley wants to say that it's hard to find room in your bag for homework when there's a monkey in there instead.

The day gets even harder when Mr Robinson asks the class to do silent reading. Marley knows he should read his book but Monkey wants to tell Marley better stories all about jungles and animals and tall trees.

It's not long before Marley realises that he has doodled Monkey's stories all over the pages of his book. Unfortunately for Marley, Mr Robinson sees his doodles and, before he knows it, he's in trouble again.

Today isn't going very well.

Finally, the bell goes for break time.

In the playground, Hannah is showing everyone her birthday present: a yellow boomerang. She shows them all how it flies through the air before coming straight back to her.

WHOOOSH!

Monkey thinks the boomerang looks like a banana. He wants to have a go. "Ooh ooh ooh!" squeals Monkey to Marley. "Grab it. Quick!"

Marley goes to grab it, but Hannah isn't ready to let go. "Get off, Marley!" she shouts.

She yanks the toy back and suddenly...

SNAP!

Everyone goes quiet when they hear the boomerang break. When Hannah looks down at her broken toy, her eyes get shiny and her face gets red. "Uh oh," Marley whispers.

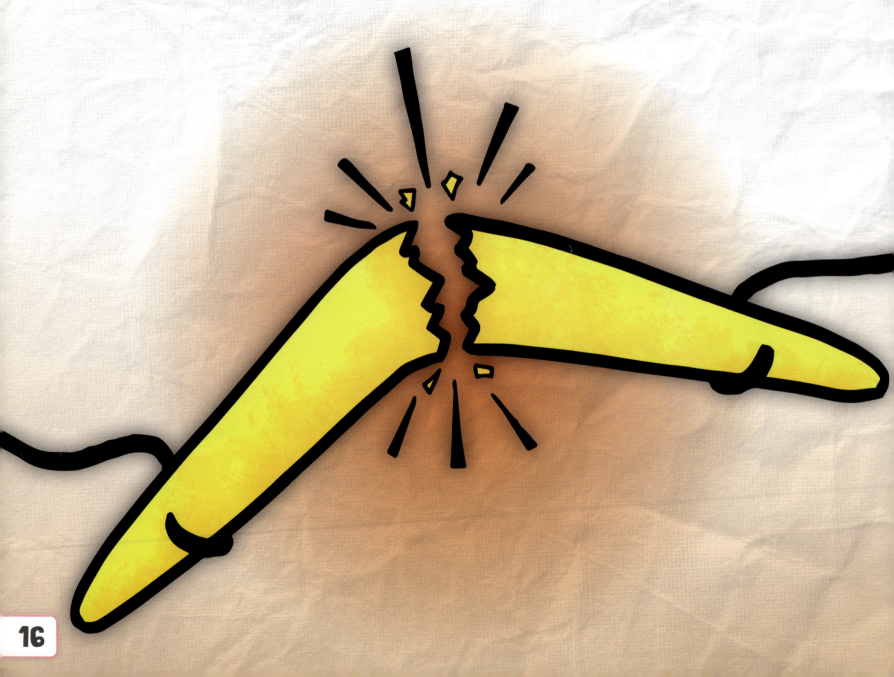

"WHAT'S GOING ON HERE?"

Monkey dives behind Marley. Suddenly he's very scared of Mr Robinson.

"Marley broke my toy," Hannah sniffles.
"It was an accident!" Marley cries.
Marley can't believe his monkey has got him in trouble again.

Inside, Mr Robinson sits a tearful Marley down at his desk. "What happened, Marley? And what's the matter?"

Marley tells his teacher all about his monkey and how he sometimes gets carried away and can't wait his turn and how he didn't mean to break Hannah's boomerang.

Marley also tells him about Monkey distracting him in silent reading and making him forget his homework. Mr Robinson looks thoughtful for a second.

"It sounds like you need a monkey expert, Marley. Luckily, I know just the person."

19

Mr Robinson takes Marley to see Linda, the school counsellor. She says she has helped lots of cheeky monkeys in her time. Linda's office has lots of toys and crayons, and a box of what she calls "fidget toys". She gives one to Marley to play with while they talk.

Linda listens to all the things Monkey makes Marley do. "He's like a bad bus driver, going the wrong way all the time," Marley says. Linda says monkeys make bad bus drivers because they are used to living in the wild where they can go wherever they like.

Linda teaches Marley how to make Monkey quieter by giving him things to play with while they work. Together they make a card that Marley can show Mr Robinson when Monkey is distracting him. Linda also helps Marley write an apology note to Hannah.

Linda says Marley might always have a cheeky monkey around but Marley doesn't mind too much. He knows where to find a marvellous monkey expert to help him when Monkey is getting out of hand!

More Information

Attention deficit hyperactivity disorder – or ADHD – is a disorder that makes people struggle with things such as staying focused, following instructions, remembering important things and sitting still. ADHD can also make people feel angry, anxious or like there is too much going on in their heads.

Lots of children struggle to pay attention from time to time, but if these problems affect your mood, school work, friendships or sleep, they might be a sign of ADHD. Talking to an adult you trust about how you feel is the first step to getting the help you need.